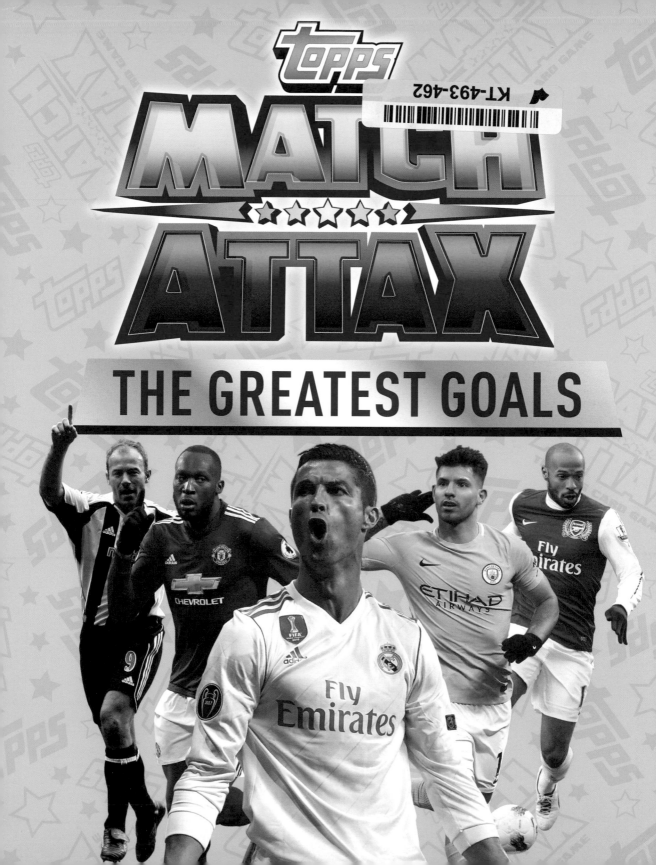

topps
MATCH ATTAX
THE GREATEST GOALS

MY GREATEST GOALS BOOK!

Your Greatest Goals book has all you need to know about footy's most epic goalscorers! It's stuffed with superstar stats, secrets and facts, plus puzzles about Premier League, Champions League and world footy goal machines. There are loads of goal tips, too, so you can score just like your heroes!

Write in your favourite goalscorers and the best goals you've ever seen, or scored, right here!

MY NAME: ....

AGE: ....

CITY/TOWN: ....

MY TOP THREE TEAMS & COUNTRIES:

1 ....

2 ....

3 ....

THE BEST GOAL EVER SCORED IS: ....

....

THE BEST GOAL I'VE EVER SCORED IS: ....

....

Barca blast the best goals!

I'VE SCORED THESE GOALS:

PENALTY ☐   FREE-KICK ☐

HEADER ☐   SHOT OUTSIDE BOX ☐

OVERHEAD KICK ☐   VOLLEY ☐

THE PREMIER LEAGUE TOP SCORER WILL BE: ....
....

THE CHAMPIONS LEAGUE TOP SCORER WILL BE: ....
....

THE CHAMPIONSHIP TOP SCORER WILL BE: ....
....

THE SCOTTISH PREMIERSHIP TOP SCORER WILL BE: ....
....

'Ave summa this!

WHAT MAKES A GREAT GOAL?

Check out these five things that help to make a goal an absolute cracker of a strike that you'll never forget!

TOP TECHNIQUE

Technique, or 'tekkers', is the level of skill, style and control you need to score. For example, an amazing dribble and finish, or an unbelievable bicycle kick, needs loads of skilful technique. Top tekkers is key to scoring a great goal!

TEAM EFFORT

Incredible individual strikes are a joy to see, but top team goals are every bit as impressive. Teams like Arsenal, Manchester City, Barcelona and Bayern Munich can crack in a well-worked team goal, and so can international sides like Spain, Brazil and Argentina.

BIG GAME

Great goals can be scored in any game – even a kickabout at the park with your mates! But belting in a world-class strike in a huge game, like a Champions League final or to win the Premier League, makes a goal feel just that little bit extra special.

SUPERSTAR PLAYERS

Stars like Sergio Aguero, Eden Hazard and Cristiano Ronaldo can give a great goal an even GREATER feel – simply because they're such awesome footballers! Every fan wants to see these master goalscorers hit the net with a magical move.

Ooooh, scary face alert!

In 2017, Real Madrid's **Cristiano Ronaldo** became the first player to score in three Champions League finals.

CRAZY CELEBRATION

After scoring a great goal, fans love to see a cool celebration as well! Neymar, Ronaldo, Pierre-Emerick Aubameyang and Harry Kane have all pulled out some slick celebrations after burying the ball into the back of the net.

Check out these mega goal machines, including current strike sensations and heroes from the past. These players could find the net with their eyes closed!

GREATEST GOALSCORERS!

PELE

MAIN CLUB: Santos
COUNTRY: Brazil

- Brazil's greatest striker: 77 goals in 91 games
- Strength, speed and a great team player
- Scored 1,281 goals in the 1950s, '60s and '70s

THIERRY HENRY

MAIN CLUBS: Barcelona, Arsenal
COUNTRY: France

- Champions League, World Cup & Premier League winner
- Speedy, strong and full of tricks and flicks
- Arsenal's record goalscorer with 228 goals

LIONEL MESSI

CLUB: Barcelona
COUNTRY: Argentina

- Record scorer for Barcelona and Argentina
- Skilful, fast and a laser left foot
- Over 30 major trophies since 2005

In March 2018, **Messi** bagged his **100th** Champions League goal for Barcelona.

SERGIO AGUERO

MAIN CLUBS: Manchester City, Atletico Madrid
COUNTRY: Argentina
- Became the Citizens' top scorer in 2017 with 178th strike
- Legendary coolness in the box
- Shoots from anywhere and rarely misses the target

ALLY McCOIST

MAIN CLUB: Rangers
COUNTRY: Scotland
- Twice European Golden Boot winner in the 1990s
- Snapped up chances in the area
- Rangers' record marksman struck 355 club goals

WAYNE ROONEY

CLUBS: Everton and Manchester United
COUNTRY: England
- England's top striker with 53 from 119 games
- Manchester United legend with 253 goals
- Five Premier League and one Champions League titles

ROBERT LEWANDOWSKI

MAIN CLUBS: Bayern Munich, Borussia Dortmund
COUNTRY: Poland
- Rocket shooting and power-packed heading
- Champions League star with 45 goals in 68 games
- Scored five goals in nine minutes in 2015

Brian Munick? Never heard of him.

Lewandowski scored a record **16** goals for Poland as they qualified for the 2018 World Cup.

ALFREDO DI STEFANO

MAIN CLUB: Real Madrid
COUNTRY: Spain and Argentina
- Scored in, and won, the first five European Cup finals
- Played for both Argentina and then Spain
- Stylish striker with an epic goal instinct

HENRIK LARSSON

MAIN CLUBS: Barcelona, Celtic
COUNTRY: Sweden
- Celtic hero thanks to 242 strikes in just 315 appearances
- Clever movement, vision and speed
- Champions League winner with Barcelona in 2006

ALAN SHEARER

MAIN CLUBS: Newcastle United, Blackburn Rovers
COUNTRY: England
- Record Premier League scorer with 260 goals
- Powerful in the air, fierce shooting
- Grabbed 30 goals in just 63 England games

Shearer is one of only two players to score over **200** Premier League goals for two different clubs (Newcastle United and Blackburn Rovers).

GERD MULLER

MAIN CLUB: Bayern Munich
COUNTRY: Germany
- World Cup and Euros winner in the 1970s
- Cool instinct to be in the right place to score
- Only player to score 40 Bundesliga goals in a season

CRISTIANO RONALDO

MAIN CLUBS: Real Madrid, Manchester United
COUNTRY: Portugal
- Deadly in the box and free-kick specialist
- Portugal captain and Euro 2016 winner
- Top scorer at Real Madrid, hitting over 430 goals

Does anyone want to tickle me?

Ibrahimovic has scored for Manchester United, Paris Saint-Germain, AC Milan, Barcelona, Inter Milan, Juventus, Ajax and Malmo.

HARRY KANE

CLUB: Tottenham Hotspur
COUNTRY: England
- Multiple Premier League Golden Boot winner
- Lethal inside and outside the box
- Cracked in 100 Premier League goals in 141 matches

NEYMAR

MAIN CLUBS: Barcelona, Paris Saint-Germain
COUNTRY: Brazil
- Crazy skills, tricks and dribbling power
- League champion in France, Spain and Brazil
- Record transfer fee of £200 million in 2017

ZLATAN IBRAHIMOVIC

MAIN CLUBS: Inter Milan, Paris Saint-Germain, Manchester United
COUNTRY: Sweden
- Super strong with acrobatic finishing
- Won trophies in five countries
- Sweden's top striker with 62 goals in 116 games

BEST GOALS EVER!

Presenting the greatest Premier League goals ever scored! This is your guide to the most spectacular strikes, the net-busters and record-breakers from from every single season of the most exciting league on the planet!

I'm much better than that Harry Kane fella!

SLICK SANE

In an action-packed 4–3 defeat to Liverpool FC, Leroy Sane lashed in a terrific shot after cutting in from the wing. He beat two defenders and fired past the keeper at the near post. Quality.

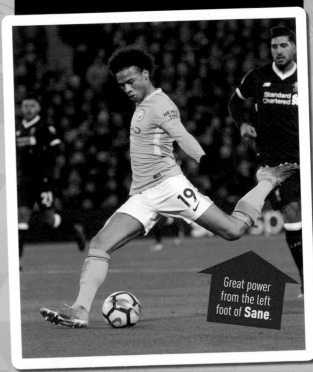

Great power from the left foot of **Sane**.

HOT TOTT!

Christian Eriksen capped off a great team move to score for Tottenham Hotspur against Everton. Heung-Min Son flicked the ball to Dele Alli, who backheeled it to Eriksen to sweep into the net.

Salah loves his left foot – **23** of his first **26** Premier League goals were scored with that boot!

GO, GO, MO!

Liverpool FC's Mo Salah began 2018 in top gear, bagging seven goals in his first nine Premier League games. His second strike against Spurs at Anfield was very special – Salah showed quick feet, close control and a cheeky finish to beat keeper Hugo Lloris.

CAN'S CANNONBALL

The No.1 Premier League goal in 2017 was Emre Can's brilliant bicycle kick for Liverpool FC against Watford. Struck from just inside the box, his high right-foot shot flew into the top corner. It was the winning goal, too!

Amazing acrobatic skill!

So far, so good for super Sof!

In 2017 **Can** also scored his first goal for Germany with a long-range hit against Azerbaijan.

SOLO STRIKE

Southampton star Sofiane Boufal scored a cracking solo goal after dribbling past five West Bromwich Albion players and stroking the ball into the net.

ROO BEAUTY

Everton's Wayne Rooney completed his hat-trick against West Ham United with a stunning shot from inside his own half!

DELE'S DELIGHT

In January 2016, Dele Alli scored one of the best goals of his life for Tottenham Hotspur against Crystal Palace. The midfield magician controlled the ball on the edge of the box, flicked it over his head and lashed a lethal spinning volley into the net!

ALLI'S SPURS' GOALS
2015: **4**
2016: **13**
2017: **23**

COOL KANE

This was another spectacular Spurs goal in 2016. Harry Kane curled a wonder strike from the edge of the box against rivals Arsenal!

VARDY'S VOLLEY

What a special strike this was against Liverpool FC! Jamie Vardy let a long pass from Riyad Mahrez bounce in front of him, before bending in a fierce volley from miles outside the box.

> Great technique, making the ball swerve into the goal

CHARLIE'S CHELSEA STUNNER

In 2015, Stoke star Charlie Adam stunned Stamford Bridge with a brilliant goal from near the centre circle. The former Liverpool FC midfielder fired a left-foot smasher high over the reach of goalkeeper Thibaut Courtois. Amazing!

In his first Premier League season in 2010–11, **Adam** hit an impressive **12** goals for Blackpool.

MATA'S MAGIC

Manchester United midfielder Juan Mata pulled off a magic trick with an eye-popping volley against Liverpool FC at Anfield.

> Trick-tastic!

> **Mata** watched the ball closely.

SNEAKY SANCHEZ

Alexis Sanchez scored a sneaky flicked goal against Manchester United for Arsenal in 2015. Just over two years later, the Gunner became a Red Devil!

You won't stop this, keeper!

Barkley showed epic close control and skill.

SHELVEY SMASHES IT

Swansea City's Jonjo Shelvey lit up the Premier League with an ace goal against Aston Villa. He took the ball in the centre circle and smashed a powerful laser-like lob straight over keeper Brad Guzan.

SHELVEY'S PREMIER LEAGUE GOAL STATS
Right foot: **83%**
Left foot: **17%**
Header: **0%**

BARKLEY'S BEST

Playing for Everton against QPR, Ross Barkley played a one-two pass in the middle of the pitch, then raced forward to lash a beauty past the keeper!

SILVA SHINES

Manchester City's David Silva jinked past two West Ham United midfielders before curling a low left-foot drive into the net at Upton Park!

SPOT THE STRIKERS

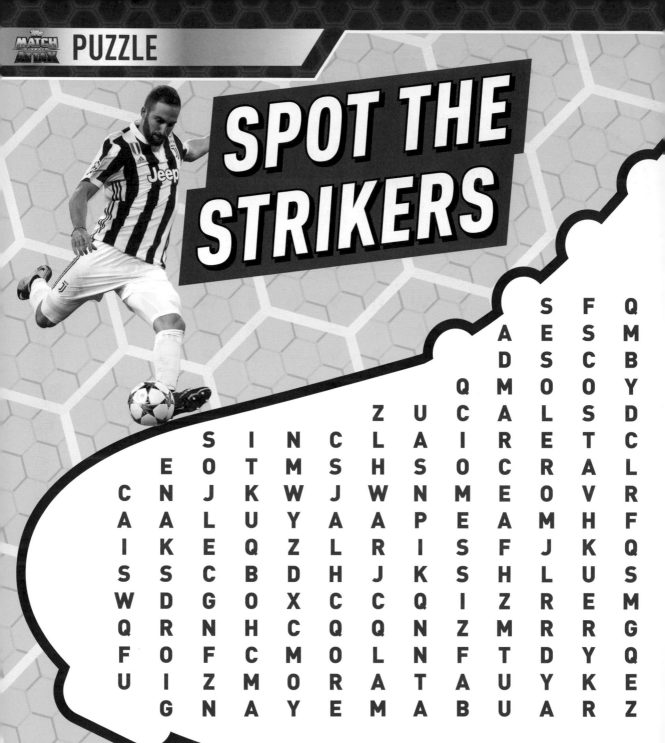

```
                                            S       F   Q
                          A         E   S   F   S   C   Q   M
                          D     M   O       O           B
                    Q     A     L       S           Y
              Z  U        C     A   R           E   T       D
        S  I  N  C  L  A  I  R  O       C       A   V   C
     E  O  T  M  S  H  S  O  E          R       A   H   L
  C  N  J  K  W  J  W  N  M  C       R  V          R
  A  A  L  U  Y  A  A  P  E  A          O       H   F
  I  K  E  Q  Z  L  R  I  S          M  J       K   Q
  S  S  C  B  D  H  J  K  S          F  L       U   S
  W  D  G  O  X  C  C  Q  H          J  R       E   M
  Q  R  N  H  C  C  Q  Q  N       Z  L  R          R  G
  F  O  F  C  M  O  L  N  I       M  R             D  Y  Q
  U  I  Z  M  M  O  R  A  T    F  T  U             Y  K  G
     G  N  A  Y  E  M  A  B    A  U  A             R  Z
```

Can you find these goal kings hiding in the boot?

KANE	MESSI	SINCLAIR
HIGUAIN	FIRMINO	VARDY
RONALDO	COSTA	GRIEZMANN
NEYMAR	MORATA	AGUERO
MORELOS	SANCHEZ	AUBAMEYANG
BENZEMA	CAVANI	

Atletico Madrid's **Griezmann** bagged the Golden Boot for France at UEFA Euro 2016 with six goals.

```
X G Q N G W O V D A W
D H I G U A I N S A C Y
C G Q N G M O V V A R N
T P M C R M S A N C H E Z
D L Q I E C U I B L S T N
N R B S I S B R X J J D O
N R G A X Z A O N I M R I F
L B O V M C P S O Q B H A
Q K B E A A L L N R I S X
A F Y H N V O R E U G A X
T A G E N A P G Y R P R K
N A M E Z N E B M D G U Q
O A H Y M I F C A U I W Y
U R J Q Z V C R R Y P A T
M B A P Y J F V P Q V E D
S X X T Y Y B B C F O B
```

Great passing movement!

JACK IN THE BOX

The best Premier League goal in 2013 has to be Jack Wilshere's wonderful team goal for Arsenal against Norwich City. The Gunners popped the ball around, before Olivier Giroud flicked it into Wilshere's path in the box and he finished with ease!

BALE FORCE!

Gareth Bale was unstoppable for Tottenham Hotspur. In January 2013 he finished a powerful solo run from the centre circle with a belting finish!

Wilshere scored his first goals for England in his 28th appearance. He blasted twice from distance against Slovenia in 2015.

REDS' ROCKET

Liverpool FC's Luis Suarez scored an unbelievable 12 goals in just six games against Norwich City. His best was a long-range screamer in December 2013 that looped into the net.

VICIOUS VOLLEY

Towering goal machine Peter Crouch has scored over 50 headers in the Premier League. But, this time it was his feet that did the talking with a sweet volley volley for Stoke City against Manchester City!

ZERO PENALTIES ZERO FREE-KICKS

Crouch has never scored from a penalty or free-kick in the Premier League!

Fierce strike surprised the keeper!

Big Pete does the business!

TAARABT TRICKERY

QPR fans remember Adel Taarabt as a tricky and skilful goalscorer. They will never forget this mazy run and curling strike against West Ham United.

PERFECT PAPISS

Striker Papiss Cisse scored 37 goals in 117 games at Newcastle United – and this was the best of the bunch! Against Chelsea, Cisse smacked a snap shot from the edge of the box that curled and cruised past Petr Cech. Stamford Bridge was totally stunned by it!

WAYNE'S WONDER STRIKE

Wayne Rooney makes his second appearance in this best Premier League goal round-up. This time he flies through the air and sends a superb volley past Joe Hart to win the Manchester derby. Unforgettable!

VAN THE MAN

Robin van Persie pulled off a brilliant angled volley in the box for Arsenal against Everton. It was just two weeks before Christmas – the perfect present for Gunners fans!

Merry Goal-mas!

CARLOS KICKS OFF!

This fantastic free-kick by Carlos Tevez had power, swerve and bags of style! The Argentine ace got his fans rocking with this outrageous goal in 2011.

TEVEZ'S PREMIER LEAGUE GOAL STATS

West Ham United: **7**
Manchester United: **19**
Manchester City: **58**

TOP TORRES!

Fernando Torres was awesome for Liverpool FC, scoring 65 Premier League goals in just 102 games. His curling shot from the edge of the box against Sunderland was pure class – Torres was a red-hot star at Anfield!

TORRES' PREMIER LEAGUE GOAL STATS

Right foot: **71%**
Left foot: **12%**
Header: **17%**

BOLT FROM THE BLUE!

Powerhouse Chelsea defender Alex bashed a free-kick straight past Lukasz Fabianski. The Arsenal keeper had zero chance of stopping the thunderbolt!

TOM'S TOP SCORE

Most of Tom Huddlestone's Totttenham goals were power-packed strikes from outside the box. One rocket shot against Bolton nearly bust the net!

FIGUEROA FLIES IN

Maynor Figueroa was a tough-tackling midfielder for Wigan Athletic, but in 2009 he caused a stir with the best goal of the year! His quick free-kick from inside his own half sailed over the Stoke City team and into the net. Big up, Fig!

KONCHESKY'S CRACKER

Playing against his former club West Ham United, Fulham left-back Paul Konchesky fired an unstoppable shot from outside the box. His left foot became a rocket launcher in that game!

DOUBLED UP

Manchester City lost 4–3 to Manchester United, but Craig Bellamy scored two beauties for The Citizens. His first was a right-footed net-buster from distance.

Bellamy has hit the net for **seven** Premier League clubs – Cardiff City, Liverpool FC, Manchester City, West Ham United, Blackburn Rovers, Newcastle United and Coventry City.

RON'S MEGA MISSILE

Manchester United's Cristiano Ronaldo fired an out-of-this-world free-kick against Portsmouth at Old Trafford! Like a guided missile, the ball swerved and spun – fans couldn't believe what had happened. It was Ronaldo's second goal in three minutes.

Ronaldo scored **nine** free-kicks and **11** penalties in the Premier League for Manchester United between 2003 and 2009.

Ronaldo struck from his laces!

See you later. Mr Ball!

POMPEY PILEDRIVER

Right-back Glen Johnson scored a goal that Ronaldo would have been proud of! He chested the ball while running and thumped a left-foot volley right past Hull City's goalkeeper. Class!

GEO BLAST

One of the most incredible goals in 2008 was when Hull's Brazilian midfielder Geovanni blasted a shot from outside the box at Arsenal. It helped The Tigers win 2–1.

Hands up if you're a Boro hero?

AWESOME ADEBAYOR

In the North London derby against Tottenham Hotspur, Emmanuel Adebayor created a magical goal that Arsenal fans will never forget. He flicked the ball up on the edge of the box, turned, and bashed a belting volley as The Gunners won 3–1.

ADEBAYOR'S PREMIER LEAGUE GOAL STATS

Arsenal: **46**
Manchester City: **15**
Tottenham Hotspur: **35**
Crystal Palace: **1**

TUNCAY TURNS IT ON

Turkish hero Tuncay finished with a smart side-footed volley to beat Derby County 1–0 at Pride Park. It was his third goal in three games for Middlesbrough during December 2007.

RONALDO & ROONEY

Wayne Rooney and Cristiano Ronaldo were a devastating double-act at Manchester United. In 2007, Rooney finished with a clever chip in the box after Ronaldo raced away to set him up.

Get in the net!

BOLTON BELTER

Nicolas Anelka's dipping long shot for Bolton Wanderers was special for many reasons. It was the best Premier League goal of 2006, his first league goal for the club – and it was against his old team, Arsenal!

ROBIN TO THE RESCUE

Robin van Persie grabbed another of the Premier League's greatest goals – the Dutchman rose high to smack a superb volley against Charlton Athletic as Arsenal came from behind to win 2–1.

Anelka won the title with Arsenal and Chelsea and took the Premier League Golden Boot in 2009 with **19** goals.

SUPER SOLANO

Newcastle United supporters loved watching flying winger Nolberto Solano curl a great strike past Everton. He flicked the ball with his right foot and it bent into the goal as if by magic!

PRECISE PEDERSEN

Morten Gamst Pedersen unleashed one of the best Premier League goals at Ewood Park with a fierce volley. He met a cross in the box and whacked it home past Fulham keeper Tony Warner.

VIEIRA'S PREMIER LEAGUE STATS

Games: **307**
Goals: **31**
Passes: **881**
Assists: **34**
Yellow cards: **76**
Red cards: **8**

PAT PACKS A PUNCH

Patrick Vieira was one of Arsenal's best captains, winning three Premier League titles and three FA Cups. The big Frenchman finished a fine passing move with a clever chipped goal in a 7–0 win over Everton!

GREAT GREEK

In 2005, Bolton had a goalscoring Greek called Stelios Giannakopoulos starring in their midfield. His well-worked power-packed goal against Norwich City was very special!

STORM THE PALACE

At the start of the 2004–05 season, Aston Villa's Lee Hendrie cracked in a corking goal against Crystal Palace! His quick footwork took the ball away from the opposition and he then thumped a thunderbolt past the keeper!

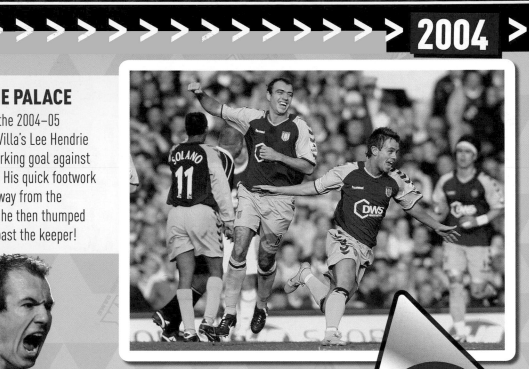

That was a red-hot Robben rocket!

ALONSO'S ARROW

Liverpool FC's Xabi Alonso fired a brilliant shot with the outside of his right foot to help beat Arsenal. It came after a great counter-attacking move from The Reds!

Hendrie joined Aston Villa when he was still at school and played his first Premier League game for the club aged **18**.

TEAM TIME

Chelsea fans were treated to a top team goal during their 4–0 win against Norwich City. Arjen Robben pounced on a brilliant back-heeled pass from Tiago and tucked it away with great skill!

Answer these cool questions to find out which Premier League goal hero you're most like!

WHICH GOALSCORER ARE YOU?

NO

Do you usually take **penalties** for your team?

YES

START

Does your game use **speed and vision**, or are you a **powerful player** who battles defenders?

SPEED

POWER

Do you often try to score from **free-kicks**?

YES

NO

Watford striker **Troy Deeney** has scored over 100 times for the Hornets.

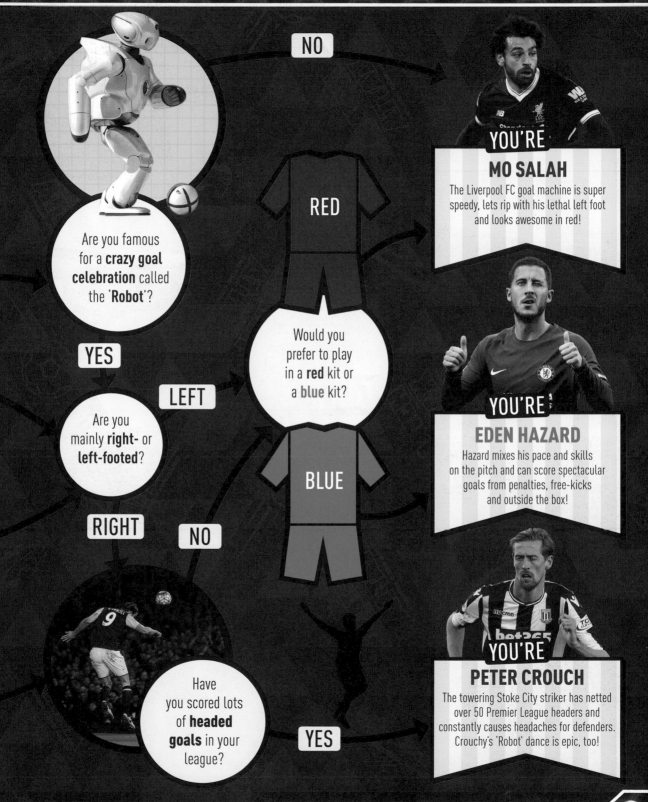

Are you famous for a **crazy goal celebration** called the 'Robot'?

NO

YES

Are you mainly **right-** or **left-footed**?

LEFT

RIGHT

NO

RED

Would you prefer to play in a **red** kit or a **blue** kit?

BLUE

Have you scored lots of **headed goals** in your league?

YES

YOU'RE

MO SALAH

The Liverpool FC goal machine is super speedy, lets rip with his lethal left foot and looks awesome in red!

YOU'RE

EDEN HAZARD

Hazard mixes his pace and skills on the pitch and can score spectacular goals from penalties, free-kicks and outside the box!

YOU'RE

PETER CROUCH

The towering Stoke City striker has netted over 50 Premier League headers and constantly causes headaches for defenders. Crouchy's 'Robot' dance is epic, too!

ICE-COOL EIDUR

Iceland star, Eidur Gudjohnsen, scored 54 Premier League goals at Chelsea. His ultimate strike was an an unbelievable overhead kick against Leeds United at Stamford Bridge.

RUUD RIPS IT UP

The No.1 goal in 2003 was easily Ruud van Nistelrooy's magical move and finish for Manchester United! He took the ball in the centre circle, turned, raced towards goal, beat four players and shot low past the Fulham goalkeeper. Sweet!

FANTASTIC FREE-KICK

Before Geremi won two titles with Chelsea, he was a midfield powerhouse for Middlesbrough. In 2003 he curled a great right-footed free-kick into the top corner at Liverpool FC.

VAN NISTELROOY'S EPIC 2002–03 SEASON
Premier League goals: **25**
Golden Boot ✔
Title winner ✔
Player of the Season ✔

SHEARER STRIKES AGAIN

This could be Alan Shearer's finest Premier League goal – and there were 260 of them in total! For Newcastle United against Everton, he blasted a supersonic volley that rocketed into the net and made everyone's jaw drop!

DEADLY DENNIS

Dennis Bergkamp showed skill, technique, quick-thinking and cool finishing with this classic strike for Arsenal against Newcastle United. He spun the ball past a defender, twisted to face the goal and conjured a breathtaking side-footed goal.

Hmmm, looks like it's going to rain...

HAMMER TIME

In a shock 3–2 win for West Ham United at Chelsea, The Hammers' captain Paolo Di Canio flicked the ball up with his right foot, then powered a left-footed volley into the net.

Di Canio's best season was in 1999–2000, with **16** Premier League goals for The Hammers.

It's the Shaun Bartlett show, folks!

BARTLETT BULLET

Charlton Athletic enjoyed playing in the Premier League between 2000 and 2006. In that time, Shaun Bartlett scored their best goal with a fantastic left-footed volley against Leicester City.

Bartlett's first two Premier League goals were against champions Manchester United in a crazy **3–3** draw.

STEVIE'S SCREAMER

All Liverpool FC players dream of scoring against rivals Manchester United at Anfield. That's exactly what boyhood Reds fan Steven Gerrard did with a long-distance blast in 2001!

NO MERCY

Aston Villa star Paul Merson bent a brilliant shot from the edge of the box to beat Coventry City. It was one of Merson's greatest Villa goals and came in a win that relegated the Sky Blues!

Di Canio struck with perfect timing.

I'm always Gunner be the best!

DERBY DELIGHT

In a London derby game against Wimbledon, West Ham United wondergoal-scorer Paolo Di Canio did the magic again! His scissor-kick volley was out of this world.

GOAL KING COLE

Manchester United striker Andrew Cole won a header just inside Coventry City's area, turned inside a defender and chipped the keeper with a cheeky dink. Unforgettable!

HENRY THE GREAT!

In an exciting Premier League battle with Manchester United, Arsenal's Thierry Henry proved what a superstar striker he was! With his back to goal on the edge of the box, he flicked the ball up, swivelled and smacked a sweet volley in the blink of an eye.

HENRY'S GOLDEN-BOOT RECORD STATS

2001–02:	**24** goals
2003–04:	**30** goals
2004–05:	**25** goals
2005–06:	**27** goals

FRENCH FLAIR

Flying Tottenham Hotspur winger David Ginola was sensational on Boxing Day in 1999! The skilful France star danced into Watford's goal, beat three players and found the bottom corner. The perfect late Christmas present for Spurs fans.

Ginola was a magical player with an incredible touch. He also starred for Newcastle United, Aston Villa and Everton.

Woo hoo! I've found my hairbrush!

GUNNERS' GREAT

Arsenal legend Emmanuel Petit only scored nine League goals in three seasons. His best was against Spurs in 1999 when he burst into the box and hooked home a great pass from Dennis Bergkamp.

BLUES SKY HIGH

Chelsea trounced Sunderland 4–0 at Stamford Bridge. When Gianfranco Zola lofted a high ball into the box, Gustavo Poyet jumped to smash an epic volley past keeper Thomas Sorensen.

FOXES' FAVE

It's another top goal for Leicester City! Midfield master Muzzy Izzet buried a right-footed volley from outside the area to bag the second goal in a 2–1 win against Spurs.

FAB FROGGATT

Left-winger Steve Froggatt scored a solo Premier League goal for Coventry City in the 1998–99 season – but it was a scorcher! Against Everton, he ran with the ball from his own half and cranked it into the top corner at about 3,000 mph!

HESKEY HITS THE CHAMPS

Emile Heskey became a big hero at Leicester City in the late 1990s, thanks to goals like this cracker against Arsenal! The Premier League champions couldn't handle Heskey's power and pace as he charged forwards and hit a low drive past keeper David Seaman.

HUNDRED-CLUB HESKEY

Heskey is one of a select group of players to have scored over 100 Premier League goals. By April 2018, just 28 players had reached that mark.

Games: **516**   Goals: **110**

I'll 'kamp' out in the penalty box!

ZOLA GOAL-A!

Chelsea had lots of world-class international stars in the 1990s and Gianfranco Zola was the best of the best! His driving and dazzling run produced a great goal after just two minutes against Manchester United.

DAVIES' DEBUT

The 1997–98 season was Kevin Davies' first in the Premier League. In November the powerful forward hit the goal of his life with a solo run from his own half, beating four Everton players before drilling the ball into the net.

Bergkamp bagged the Premier League Player of the Month prize in August and September **1997**.

HAT-TRICK STAR

Arsenal's Dennis Bergkamp hit so many amazing goals! In 1997 he blasted a hat-trick at Leicester City and for his third strike he controlled a high pass in the box, brought it down and side-footed it past the stunned Foxes keeper. Absolute quality!

BERGKAMP'S TOP THREE PREMIER LEAGUE SEASONS

1997–98: **16** goals
1996–97: **12** goals
1998–99: **12** goals

BECKHAM BLAST

Manchester United winger David Beckham showed off his skill and style with a classy finish in August 1996. On the halfway line, Becks floated the ball over the Wimbledon defence and goalkeeper – and then celebrated like a proper superstar!

BECKHAM'S PREMIER LEAGUE STATS
Games: **265**
Goals: **62**
Assists: **80**
Titles: **6**

Beckham is the only England player to score at three World Cups, in 2006, 2002 and 1998.

MAINE MAN KINKLADZE

Georgi Kinkladze lit up Manchester City's Maine Road stadium between 1995 and 1998. His best Premier League goal for The Citizens was a waltzing run against Southampton, beating three players and then chipping the goalkeeper!

KING CANTONA

Time for another memorable Manchester United goal! Against Sunderland, captain Eric Cantona started an attack, ran into the box and chipped the keeper with a fantastic touch.

I'm Rover the moon with that goal!

Collymore also scored 26 league goals in two seasons at Liverpool FC.

AWESOME ALAN

Here's another classic strike from Alan Shearer. Playing for Blackburn Roves against Tottenham Hotspur, he found space on the edge of the area and turned to fire past Spurs' defence!

LEEDS THE WAY

Ghana striker Tony Yeboah scored some spectacular strikes for Leeds United. His No.1 goal came against Wimbledon. Yeboah took two touches with the ball in the air, drove into the box and thumped a shot in off the crossbar. Mesmerizing stuff!

SUPER STAN

In 1995, Nottingham Forest's Stan Collymore capped a terrific season with 22 Premier League goals. His best for the club was a superb solo run and goal at Crystal Palace.

YEBOAH'S LEEDS UNITED STATS

Premier League games: **47**
Premier League goals: **24**

Le Tissier also created **64** Premier League goals and was twice voted as the Player of the Month.

MATT FINISH

Southampton striker Matt Le Tissier played his whole career with the club, scoring 100 Premier League goals. Many of them were super special – just like his clever run, dribble and long-range finish at Blackburn Rovers in 1994!

COLE GOES CRAZY

As well as winning titles with Manchester United, Andy Cole also scored 43 Premier League goals in 58 games at Newcastle United. His power-packed strike against Chelsea in 1994 showed what a star he was!

WRIGHT ON

Arsenal's Ian Wright struck goal after goal after goal in the 1990s! The red-hot striker bagged a hat-trick at Southampton in 1994, with his second goal a crisp volley in the box.

DWIGHT ON!

Dwight Yorke's goal for Aston Villa against Sheffield Wednesday was more about a great team move than his tap in at the post. Aston Villa made over ten passes around the team before a cross into the box for Yorke to pounce.

FLYIN' RYAN

He was still only 19, but Manchester United's wicked winger Ryan Giggs fired in a fantastic free-kick against Blackburn Rovers in 1993. The Red Devils won the first Premier League title that year, too, and Giggs finished the season with nine goals!

Giggs won a record **13** Premier League titles with Manchester United between 1993 and 2013.

GOALSCORER GOSS

Norwich City's Jeremy Goss became a Premier League hero in 1993, thanks to fantastic goals like this volley in a 4–0 win against Leeds United. The Welshman scored six in total in the 1993–94 season.

The most goals **Southgate** scored in a Premier League season was three!

LES LASHES IT

Les Ferdinand scored 149 Premier League goals for six different clubs, but it all began at QPR. In 1992 he produced an amazing strike against Sheffield United after dribbling from the halfway line and blasting home!

SOUTHGATE STUNNER

Gareth Southgate started his Premier League career at Crystal Palace in 1992. On the first day of the season, the midfielder bent in a right-footed half volley from outside Blackburn Rovers' box.

This goal will be all Dwight!

Aston Villa finished second in the 1992–93 season, which is their highest-ever final position.

DALIAN DELIVERS!

In 1992, the year the Premier League began, Aston Villa's Dalian Atkinson created a cracking goal from nothing. Against Wimbledon he won the ball inside Aston Villa's half, skipped past three defenders and lobbed the keeper perfectly.

GOAL GUESSING

Take a look at these awesome action shots and work out whether or not a goal was scored!

Wait for the whistle!

1

Celtic's Callum McGregor charges towards Bayern Munich's goal.

IT WAS A GOAL.

IT WASN'T A GOAL.

Manchester City beat Leicester City 5–1, but did Sergio Aguero score here?

IT WAS A GOAL.

IT WASN'T A GOAL.

2

Chelsea's Olivier Giroud shoots through a crowd of West Bromwich Albion players here.

IT WAS A GOAL.

IT WASN'T A GOAL.

4

Christian Benteke takes aim for Crystal Palace against Everton.

IT WAS A GOAL.

IT WASN'T A GOAL.

Barcelona's Luis Suarez blasts towards Real Madrid goalkeeper Keylor Navas.

IT WAS A GOAL.

IT WASN'T A GOAL.

5

ANSWERS ON PAGE 94.

Scoring a goal is the best thing in footy, but bustin' out a mega celebration is also extremely epic!

CRAZY CELEBRATIONS

This game sucks!

Thumb-thing is wrong with **Mesut Ozil**!

Another six goals to go with my six-pack!

Crash landing alert! Crash landing alert!

Firmino kicks off!

Ronaldo muscles in for Real Madrid!

5 WAYS TO...
BEAT THE KEEPER

He's made me look a proper muppet!

Take in these top tips on how to outsmart the keeper. You'll soon be a big danger in front of goal, just like these stars!

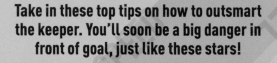

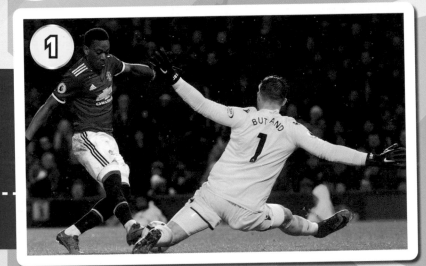

If the goalkeeper goes to ground early to block your shot, lift the ball over him and into the goal. To chip, make contact with the ball using the inside toe part of your boot.

JUST LIKE... Anthony Martial
(Manchester United)

Using quick footwork, take the ball one way and then quickly back the other. The keeper could wrongly dive to one side and give you a great chance to score!

JUST LIKE... Jamie Vardy
(Leicester City)

3

The most difficult spot for a keeper to reach is usually the bottom corners. Aim your shots and headers here and you'll have a better chance of finding the net.

JUST LIKE... Jermain Defoe
(AFC Bournemouth)

If you always hang around just in front of the goal defenders can easily mark you. Keep moving and make late runs into the box, then surprise the keeper with a quick-fire shot.

JUST LIKE... David Silva
(Manchester City)

4

Cech out my skills, Petr!

5

Even when keepers make easy saves or goal kicks, it's a good idea to be alert and stay close to them. Sometimes they will drop the ball or kick it into your path – and that means a simple goal for you!

JUST LIKE... Jordan Ayew
(Swansea City)

> Praise be to. er…me!

ULTIMATE
CHAMPIONS
LEAGUE STRIKES

It's the greatest European club competition, and these are the greatest goals it has ever seen!

LIONEL MESSI

Real Madrid v BARCELONA
April 27, 2011

- Fine solo goal against Barca's biggest rivals
- Messi dribbled past four players into the box
- Clever finish, even with his weaker right foot!

CRISTIANO RONALDO

Liverpool v REAL MADRID
October 22, 2014

- Great team move by Real Madrid at Anfield
- Ronaldo collected a ball scooped into the box
- Accurate right-foot finish from the striker

PETER CROUCH
LIVERPOOL FC v Galatasaray, 2006
Brilliant overhead kick.

ALEKSANDR RYAZANTSEV
Barcelona v RUBIN KAZAN, 2009
Fierce drive in a famous 2–1 win.

ALESSANDRO FLORENZI

ROMA v Barcelona
September 16, 2015

- The Italian raced down the right wing from his own half
- He spotted the Barca keeper off his line and chipped the ball in from 45 metres out (about 50 yards)

It's easy peasy for Zizou!

ROBERT LEWANDOWSKI

BORUSSIA DORTMUND v Real Madrid
April 24, 2013

- Lewandowski completed his hat-trick with neat finish in the box
- He cleverly dragged the ball away from defender Pepe
- First to score four in a Champions League semi-final

DEJAN STANKOVIC

INTER MILAN v Schalke
April 5, 2011

- Stankovic met the goalkeeper's clearance in the centre circle
- He volleyed it back into Schalke's goal with power
- Scored in the first minute, but Inter lost 5–2

ZINEDINE ZIDANE

Bayer Leverkusen v REAL MADRID
May 15, 2002

- One of the best Champions League final goals
- Zidane struck an awesome left-foot volley from outside the box
- The goal sealed a brilliant 2–1 victory for Real Madrid

EMMANUEL ADEBAYOR
Liverpool FC v ARSENAL, 2008
Cool finish from Theo Walcott's assist.

MAURO BRESSAN
FIORENTINA v Barcelona, 1999
Expert overhead kick from outside the box.

Watch out – this one's going in the top corner!

ZLATAN IBRAHIMOVIC

Anderlecht v PARIS SAINT-GERMAIN

October 23, 2013

- Ibrahimovic raced onto a loose ball outside the box
- Stunning swerving shot from the PSG captain
- The striker scored four goals against Anderlecht

CRISTIANO RONALDO

Porto v MANCHESTER UNITED

April 15, 2009

- A long-distance rocket from Ronaldo
- The ball flew into the top corner
- This winning goal took them into the semi-finals

LUIS SUAREZ

BARCELONA v Arsenal

March 16, 2016

- Acrobatic volley by Suarez at Camp Nou
- Dani Alves whipped a cross into the box
- Suarez soared to strike the ball into the top corner

DEJAN SAVICEVIC
AC MILAN v Barcelona, 1994
Looping long range finish in 4–0 win.

DAVIDE ZAPPACOSTA
CHELSEA v Qarabag, 2017
Lofted shot from the touchline.

THIERRY HENRY

Real Madrid v ARSENAL
February 21, 2006

- Henry picked the ball up in the centre circle at the Bernabeu
- He raced past four players with power and expert dribbling
- Blasted a low shot as Arsenal won 1–0

PHILIPPE MEXES

Anderlecht v AC MILAN
November 21, 2011

- Amazing overhead kick by France centre-back Mexes
- He chested the ball on the edge of Anderlecht's box
- Superb technique to fire a right-footed volley into the net

Arsenal reached their only Champions League final in **2006**, but lost to Barcelona.

MARIO MANDZUKIC

JUVENTUS v Real Madrid
June 3, 2017

- Unbelievable overhead volley in the Champions League final
- Sandro volleyed to Higuan in the box, who set up Mandzukic
- The Croatian chested the ball and struck an acrobatic shot

KAKA
Manchester United v AC MILAN, 2007
Powerful run and drive in the box.

ANTOINE GRIEZMANN
ATLETICO MADRID v Roma, 2017
Outrageous left-footed volley.

Topps MATCH ATTAX

PLAY TO WIN!

As every football manager knows, you need strategy as well as top players to be a winner. Here are five top tips to help you collect and play like a pro. You'll soon be a Match Attax master!

I'm a hat-trick hero!

100 Club

101

101

1 101 – THE ULTIMATE MATCH ATTAX CARD

Look out for the new 101-rated card in packets. The 101-er is unbeatable so it's a no-brainer to get one into your line-up!

2 AWAY KITS AND HAT-TRICK HEROES!

Away Kit cards feature players in their team's alternative strip and are a must-have for your team. These cool cards could score you two goals meaning playing away from home need never be a problem again. Also don't miss out on Hat-Trick Heroes, exclusively available in Match Attax Extra, featuring players who've scored trebles throughout the season. They could score you three goals!

3 SUPER SUBS!

Each team has 11 players and three subs so if you want to switch things up, you'll need a good impact player coming off the bench. You can surprise an opponent and turn the game to your favour with a well-timed sub!

NEW MATCH ATTAX APP!

④ TALKING TACTICS

Change the game with Tactic cards. These super collectable game-changers include injury, referee and agent cards. They can damage an opponent's score, increase your transfer budget, make an opponent swap their player and even boost your cards. You're allowed to use two of them in each match so get them into your squad to take the win!

It's time to up your game!

You can now get the new Match Attax app to collect, swap and play with thousands of other fans! All you need to do is:

STEP 1: Search PL Match Attax on your App store.

STEP 2: Download the new Match Attax App.

STEP 3: Scan codes found in Match Attax packets to get free digital cards.

STEP 4: Build your digital team and join the fun!

Download on the **App Store**   GET IT ON **Google Play**

⑤ ATTACKING DEFENDERS, DEFENSIVE ATTACKERS!

Look out for players who are good in attack and defence, mainly all-rounder midfielders and flying full-backs like Paul Pogba and Marcos Alonso. These guys can spring a surprise on an opponent out of nowhere!

SWAP & PLAY TOUR

If you want to find out more about Match Attax, come along to one of our Swap & Play Tour events. You'll be able to swap cards to complete your collection, play games against other collectors and even take part in the Match Attax World Championships!

For more information about dates and events go to toppsfootball.com

These super strikes are every bit as good as the goals Kane, Ronaldo and Messi score! Check out some of the top women's goals of all time...

WOMEN'S WONDER GOALS

I've Scott a lot of goals!

CARLI LLOYD

The goalscoring midfielder was crowned Best FIFA Women's Player in 2016. Her hat-trick goal for the USA against Japan in the 2015 World Cup final saw her expertly lob the ball from the halfway line!

ALEX SCOTT

In 2007, the Arsenal right-back lashed an incredible effort to win the UEFA Women's Cup against Umea. She took two touches as she drove forwards before striking a rising shot that the keeper had no chance of saving!

Marta has scored a record **15** goals at the Women's World Cup finals.

MARTA'S SMARTS

One of the best female players ever, Marta has scored over 100 goals for Brazil. In 2007, playing against the USA, she flicked the ball past a defender, sped into the area and struck a low right-foot shot beyond the keeper. A clever goal.

STEPHANIE ROCHE

Roche belted a beauty for Peamount United against Wexford Youths in 2017. She took two touches with the ball in the air before turning to volley home. This sensational strike was awarded runner-up in FIFA's Goal of the Year!

ELLEN WHITE

In 2011, England's Ellen White struck a sweet volley against Japan. The forward let the ball bounce and with two defenders close to her, she hit the perfect volley from outside the box and over the keeper.

MARTA (AGAIN!)

Marta is such a red-hot goal machine, she deserves another mention! Her goal for Santos against Juventus in 2011 saw her waltz past three players, go round the keeper and hit the net with a cheeky flick on the goal line. Total class from a total star!

SCOTTISH PREMIERSHIP

BEST GOALS EVER!

Hold tight – you're about to read about some of the finest goals ever in Scotland's top league!

LEGENDARY LARSSON

Henrik Larsson
CELTIC v Rangers

In a huge 6–2 win over rivals Rangers, Larsson's goal was the pick of the six! The speedy striker skipped past two tackles and then lobbed the keeper with a clever dink. It was an unforgettable effort from the popular star.

YES HE KAN

Andrei Kanchelskis
Dunfermline v RANGERS

The skilful winger played 113 games and scored 19 goals for Rangers, with the best being a world-class volley at Dunfermline. Rod Wallace crossed the ball and Kanchelskis let it drop before a sweet hit sent it flying into the net!

CHRISTIE CURLER

Ryan Christie
ABERDEEN v Motherwell

This was a curling, classy finish in the box by Christie. Aberdeen took a quick corner, worked the ball to Christie who bent it into the top corner with a first-time flick with the outside of his boot!

Henrik Larsson was the league's top scorer **five** times.

Picked that one out!

GOAL GREATS

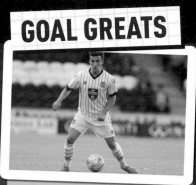

TOP TEEN

Stephen Mallan
Dundee v ST MIRREN

The 18-year-old midfielder shot to fame with a superb solo strike at Dens Park. Mallan won the ball in the centre circle, skipped through four challenges and then whacked it past the keeper from outside the box.

COUL GOAL

Souleymane Coulibaly
Celtic v KILMARNOCK

The former Spurs youth-team player spent one season at Kilmarnock, but the fans will never forget his goal at Celtic Park in 2016. He cut inside his marker and smashed an unstoppable shot, which dipped over keeper de Vries.

> Mate, how much do you weigh?

BRILLIANT BHOYS

Moussa Dembele
St Johnstone v CELTIC

Dembele's delightful finish in 2017 was the ultimate team goal! The entire Celtic team touched the ball in the build-up, with 24 passes – including a rabona and a backheeled flick – before Dembele coolly slotted it home to complete his hat-trick.

SCOT THE LOT!

Take a closer look at the biggest league in Scotland and discover the stats and facts behind its goalscoring greats.

DOUBLE TROUBLE

In 2018, a pair of experienced Scottish Premiership goal masters were still causing havoc in the league. Kilmarnock's Kris Boyd is the SPFL's record scorer with 167 for Killie and Rangers. Kenny Miller first played in the league in 1997 and scored his 100th Scottish league goal in 2016. The pair were strike partners at Rangers between 2008 and 2010.

Did you say we look like brothers?

CELTIC HERO

When the Scottish Premier League began in 1998, the competition's biggest star was Henrik Larsson. The Sweden striker buried 158 SPL goals before leaving The Bhoys in 2004 for Barcelona. In total he netted 242 times in just 315 Celtic appearances, picking up four league crowns, two Scottish Cups and two League Cups. He also lifted the Champions League trophy while at Barcelona. A class act.

GOAL GREATS

DEREK RIORDAN
St Johnstone,
Hibernian, Celtic

SCOTT MCDONALD
Celtic, Motherwell

JOHN HARTSON
Celtic

ADAM ROONEY
Aberdeen

PREMIERSHIP TOP SCORERS
2017 Liam Boyce, Ross County 23 GOALS
2016 Leigh Griffiths, Celtic 31 GOALS
2015 Adam Rooney, Aberdeen 18 GOALS
2014 Kris Commons, Celtic 27 GOALS

My golden
shoes are
well posh!

McCoist twice
won the Golden
Shoe as Europe's
top scorer, in 1992
and 1993.

RANGERS RECORD

With a record 355 goals for the Glasgow club, striker
Ally McCoist is a legend at Ibrox. He joined the Gers
in 1983 and won ten titles as a player and 18 major
honours overall. A livewire in the box and with a
natural instinct to hit the target, McCoist struck 28
hat-tricks for Rangers and finally left the club in 1998.
He later managed Rangers between 2011 and 2014.

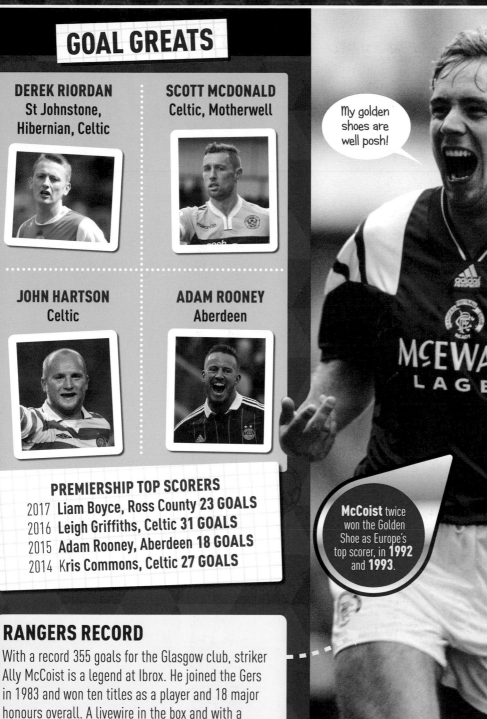

BEST GOALS EVER!

Spain's La Liga is stuffed with superstars, super teams and super-slick goals. Check out some of the best of the best!

MESSI STRIKES AGAIN!

Lionel Messi
BARCELONA v Real Sociedad

It's so tough to pick Messi's best goal in La Liga – he's scored over 375 in the competition! In 2010 he hit a mind-boggling strike against Real Sociedad after skipping past four defenders across the box and sending a low shot back across the goal.

REAL DEAL!

Raul
REAL MADRID v Real Sociedad

Real Madrid captain Raul played for 16 seasons with the club, making 741 appearances and bagging a mighty 323 goals. In 1997, the little goal machine flicked the ball over a Sociedad player, watched it drop and looped a volley past the keeper!

WICKED WILLIAMS!

Inaki Williams
ATHLETIC BILBAO v Espanyol

Goalscoring star Williams unleashed the best goal of his La Liga career against Espanyol! With his back to goal on the edge of the area, he clipped a lofted pass over two defenders and powered a precise volley into the top corner.

That was REALLY cool!

BACK IN BUSINESS!

Cristiano Ronaldo
Rayo Vallecano v REAL MADRID

As Real Madrid captured the La Liga title in 2012, star striker Ronaldo produced a moment of magic at Rayo Vallecano. About 10 metres (11 yards) from the goal line, he powered a backheel past five players and arrowed into the net.

SUPER SAUL!

Saul Berjon
EIBAR v Levante

In Eibar's first season in La Liga, skilful forward Berjon cracked in an unforgettable effort. A free-kick near the backline was floated to him just inside the area, and Berjon blasted a volley that crashed high into the net.

Just like Griez lightning!

ATLETICO ACE!

Antoine Griezmann
Real Sociedad v
ATLETICO MADRID

France forward Griezmann stunned La Liga with a top solo strike in 2015. He won the ball in the centre circle, charged forwards leaving three defenders for dust and beat the keeper with a precise left-foot finish. Amazing!

SPAIN'S STYLISH SCORERS!

If you're looking for great goals and great goal scorers, La Liga is packed with penalty box predators and action!

EL CLASICO

The biggest matches of the season are when rivals Real Madrid and Barcelona go head-to-head. These battles are called 'El Clasico' and since 2000, over 115 goals have been scored in the games. Barca won 6–2 at The Bernabeu in 2009 and stuffed them 5–0 in 2010. Real's famous 2–1 in 2012 put them seven points clear at the top of the table as they took the title. The clubs also clashed in the Champions League semi-finals in 2011 and 2002.

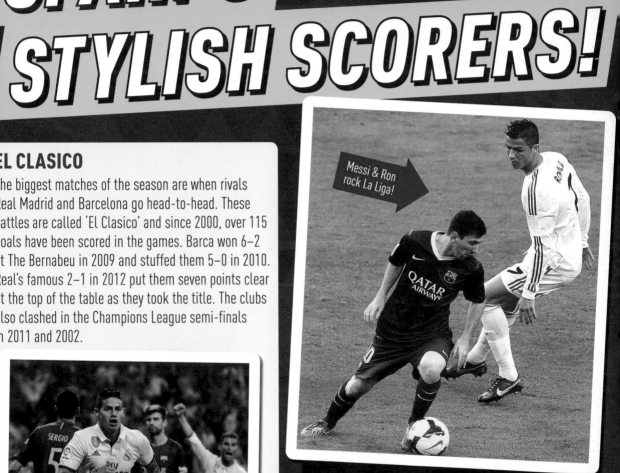

Messi & Ron rock La Liga!

RONNIE v MESSI

For the last ten years, Cristiano Ronaldo and Lionel Messi have been the best players on the planet. They've each scooped a shedload of World Player awards, league titles, Champions Leagues and golden shoe trophies. But who's the best? Ronaldo has grabbed over 400 Real Madrid goals since 2009 and Messi reached the 500 mark in 2017. It's too tough to choose the ultimate goal king in Spain!

GOAL GREATS

RUUD VAN NISTELROOY
Real Madrid & Malaga

DIEGO FORLAN
Villarreal & Atletico Madrid

MARIO KEMPES
Valencia

ROMARIO
Barcelona & Valencia

LA LIGA TOP SCORERS

2017	Lionel Messi, Barcelona	37 GOALS
2016	Luis Suarez, Barcelona	40 GOALS
2015	Cristiano Ronaldo, Real Madrid	48 GOALS
2014	Cristiano Ronaldo, Real Madrid	31 GOALS
2013	Lionel Messi, Barcelona	46 GOALS
2012	Lionel Messi, Barcelona	50 GOALS
2011	Cristiano Ronaldo, Real Madrid	40 GOALS
2010	Lionel Messi, Barcelona	34 GOALS

I eat goals for brekkie!

WORLD WONDERS

Some of football's most gifted goalscorers have busted La Liga nets since the competition began in 1929. As well as Messi and Ronaldo, goal-getters like Raul, David Villa, Samuel Eto'o, Hugo Sanchez, Alfredo Di Stefano and Ferenc Puskas have lit up games with their super strikes. Thierry Henry, Luis Suarez, Ronaldinho, Rivaldo and Ruud van Nistelrooy are more top players who've bashed in belters in Spain.

Fit these famous past and present goalscorers into each grid. Get ready for a goalmouth scramble!

GOAL GRIDS

RAUL

F O W L E R

FOWLER

SHEARER

COLE

PELE

SALAH

RONALDO

VAN PERSIE

CRUYFF

MULLER

MARADONA

LUKAKU

STERLING

KAKA

TOTTI

HENRY

PELE

BEST GOALS EVER!

Let's head to Germany to uncover the best goals ever seen in the Bundesliga. From solo stunners to ludicrous lobs, prepare to be amazed!

Defenders just can't catch Okocha!

JAY-JAY'S BIG DAY

Jay-Jay Okocha
EINTRACHT FRANKFURT v Karlsruher

Okocha's outrageously skilful goal in 1993 makes your eyes pop out of your head! The Nigerian took 11 touches in the box, twisting and turning past three defenders and then firing a low shot past keeper Oliver Kahn.

LEWANDOWSKI LATE SHOW

Robert Lewandowski
Freiburg v BAYERN MUNICH

Bayern Munich can always rely on Robert Lewandowski to deliver the goals! In the 90th minute in this Bundesliga game, the Poland striker chested the ball, controlled it with his right foot and somehow squeezed a left-footed shot home. What a dramatic winner!

WOLFSBURG WONDER STRIKE

Grafite
WOLFSBURG v Bayern Munich

When Wolfsburg won their first Bundesliga title in 2009, they thumped Bayern Munich 5–1! Brazil star Grafite dribbled into the area, coolly drifted past four players and fired a cheeky backheel past the keeper. The Volkswagen Arena went wild!

DEADLY DIEGO

Diego
WERDER BREMEN v Alemannia
In 2007, Werder Bremen midfielder Diego destroyed Alemannia with a ridiculous shot from well inside his own half. With the keeper racing back to his line, Diego chipped the ball and it dropped in the area before bouncing off the bar and into the net!

HOFF HE GOES

Takashi Usami
Stuttgart v HOFFENHEIM
Japan forward Usami only scored two Bundesliga goals for Hoffenheim, and his second in 2012 was an absolute screamer! Cutting in from the left wing, he blitzed past four challengers, cut back onto his right foot and guided the ball beyond the shocked keeper.

BREMEN BEAUTY

Mesut Ozil
Schalke v WERDER BREMEN
Ozil has hit quality goals for Arsenal and Real Madrid, but he began by bagging beauties in the Bundesliga! For Bremen in 2010, he nutmegged one player, skipped through three tackles and drove in a left-footed firecracker.

GERMANY'S GOAL-DEN BOYS!

Numbers, records, facts and figures – you'll find these, and more, all about the Bundesliga's top scorers, right here!

YEAR WE GO

The year 2017 was goal crazy in the Bundesliga! A mega 893 goals were scored in the competition across 306 games. David Alaba, Pierre-Emerick Aubameyang, Bruma and Serge Gnabry notched memorable strikes, but Bundesliga fans voted Eintracht Frankfurt striker Sebastien Haller's sensational scissor kick as the best of the year. The Frenchman flew through the air to score a 90th-minute winner against Stuttgart.

HIGH FIVE

For a striker to score five in one game is pretty special, but Robert Lewandowski did it after coming on as a half-time sub! With Bayern Munich losing 1–0 to Wolfsburg, lethal Lewie shot five goals in a record-breaking nine minutes as Bayern won 5–1. He became the highest-scoring substitute in the league and finished the season as the Bundesliga's top scorer with 30.

THOMAS MULLER
Bayern Munich

CLAUDIO PIZARRO
Cologne,
Bayern Munich,
Werder Bremen

MARIO GOMEZ
Stuttgart,
Wolfsburg,
Bayern Munich

SANDRO WAGNER
Bayern Munich

BUNDESLIGA TOP SCORERS

2017	Pierre-Emerick Aubameyang	31 GOALS
2016	Robert Lewandowski, Bayern Munich	30 GOALS
2015	Alex Meier, Eintracht Frankfurt	19 GOALS
2014	Robert Lewandowski, Borussia Dortmund	20 GOALS
2013	Stefan Kiessling, Bayer Leverkusen	25 GOALS
2012	Klaas-Jan Huntelaar, Schalke	29 GOALS
2011	Mario Gomez, Bayern Munich	28 GOALS
2010	Edin Dzeko, Wolfsburg	22 GOALS

SPEEDY STAR

As well as being a slick striker who netted 31 goals in 55 Bundesliga games for RB Leipzig, Timo Werner is also lightning fast! In the 2017–18 season, the Germany international clocked a top speed in the league of 21 mph. That was the third fastest in Germany and he makes an average of 30 sprints every game. In 2017, Werner was the highest-scoring German player, bagging 21 goals, and a third of them came from speedy counter-attacking breaks.

5 WAYS TO...
SCORE A FREE-KICK

Firing in a fab free-kick is one of the best ways to score a goal. Check out these top tips to help you become a free-kick expert.

> Practice makes perfect. Marcos!

The most important thing is to practice... a lot! At the end of your team training sessions, practice striking the ball at the goal or a target. If you can, try taking free-kicks in places like your garden and school playground to help improve your technique!

JUST LIKE... Marcos Alonso
(Chelsea)

> Add some wicked whip!

One of the best ways to hit the ball high and over a defensive wall is to strike it at the bottom, using the 'big toe' part of your boot. Stand slightly to the side of the ball and whip your foot across it.

JUST LIKE... NEYMAR
(Paris Saint-Germain)

3

Bang! What a beauty!

Sometimes if there isn't a wall to beat, or you want to surprise the keeper, you could try blasting the free-kick with power! This could be less accurate than curling a shot but the fierce strike could be too quick for the other team to stop.

JUST LIKE... Eric Dier
(Tottenham Hotspur)

Hitting a free-kick low and underneath the wall can be a sneaky way to score! The defenders and goalkeeper won't be expecting it and you can aim for the opposite part of the goal to where the keeper is standing.

JUST LIKE... Dwight Gayle
(Newcastle United)

4

Amazing acrobatic skill!

5

Even if you don't take free-kicks, it can still be a great time to score. When the kick has been taken, follow the ball into the box because you could score from a rebound or a block. All top strikers hover around the area looking for a chance!

JUST LIKE... Romelu Lukaku
(Manchester United)

BEST GOALS EVER!

Solo goals, volleys, chips, free-kicks – Italy's Serie A is packed full with fantastic and memorable strikes!

MERTENS MAGIC
Dries Mertens
NAPOLI v Torino

Dries Mertens played the game of his life when he scored four goals in Napoli's amazing 5–3 win over Torino! The Belgium forward's best strike was a smart turn and chip in the box that left the keeper stranded.

MEGA MILAN MOMENT
Jeremy Menez
Parma v AC MILAN

AC Milan fans saw one of the most skilful and cheeky goals ever in 2014! Speedy Jeremy Menez ran into the box and poked the ball past the keeper, stepped past the byline, then back on the pitch to finish with a back heel in front of the goal!

THREE FREE-KICKS
Sinisa Mihajlovic
LAZIO v Sampdoria

Mihajlovic scored a joint record 28 free-kick goals in Serie A – and three of them came in just one game! In December 1998 in Lazio's 5–2 win over Sampdoria, he hit three left-footed beauties, with the final goal a screamer from miles outside the box!

EPIC EDIN

Edin Dzeko
Inter Milan v ROMA

In 2017, Dzeko scored a cracking volley at Chelsea in the Champions League. But he struck an even better one in Serie A against Inter Milan! Dzeko trapped the ball on his chest and steered an accurate volley beyond Samir Handanovic to open the scoring.

GORGEOUS GEORGE

George Weah
AC MILAN v Verona

Even Messi and Ronaldo haven't scored like this! In 1996, AC Milan strike legend George Weah took the ball from his own penalty area, dribbled and danced past the Verona team and crashed home one of Italy's all-time top goals.

JUVE GOT IT

Zinedine Zidane
Reggina v JUVENTUS

Zidane was a ridiculously skilful and powerful player in the 1990s and 2000s, starring for Juventus, Real Madrid and France. In this Serie A game he tricked his way into the area, took out three defenders with one flick and blasted a left-footed rocket!

GOLDEN GREATS

Check out these stats and facts about the golden goalscorers who have picked up Europe's hottest striking prize – the Golden Shoe!

> I'll add this to my collection!

The **Golden Shoe** is given to the highest-scoring player in European league footy each season.

Goals scored in the big five leagues (England, Germany, France, Italy and Spain) earn two points. Each goal in smaller leagues is worth 1 or 1.5 points.

Lionel Messi won the prize for the fourth time in 2017, thanks to **37 goals** (74 points) in La Liga.

Luis Suarez scooped the European Golden Shoe in 2014 (tied with Ronaldo) and in 2016.

Cristiano Ronaldo has also racked up four Golden Shoe awards, winning in **2008**, **2011**, **2014** and **2015**.

> These are size 9, yeah?

It began in 1968, with Benfica striker **Eusebio** taking the trophy with **42** league goals.

> Portuguese master!

QUIZ FUN

SPOT THE DIFFERENCE

1 **Burnley v Manchester City** ○○○○○

2 **Everton v Crystal Palace** ○○○○○

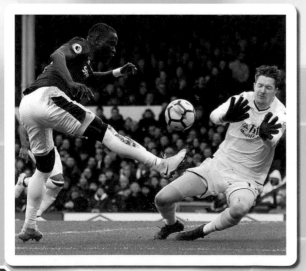

Can you spot five changes in the right-hand picture of each of these goal-crazy picture pairs?

I spotted one. do I get a prize?

③ **Bayern Munich v Hoffenheim**

④ **Real Betis v Real Madrid**

ANSWERS ON PAGE 94.

BEST GOALS EVER!

Pure worldie, that one!

France's fantastic Ligue 1 has seen plenty of quality goals. Neymar, Depay and the legendary Ibrahimovic all make this goal-crazy round-up!

PARDO ME!

Felipe Pardo
NANTES v Dijon

Pardo's perfect shot from near the corner flag capped a great 3–1 win for Nantes in Ligue 1. With the keeper off his line, Pardo cut in on his right foot and curled a delicious strike over the heads of three helpless defenders from a very tight angle.

ZLAT'S AMAZING!

Zlatan Ibrahimovic
PARIS SAINT-GERMAIN v Bastia

Zlatan Ibrahimovic blasted a mega 156 goals in just 180 games for PSG between 2012 and 2016. One of the finest was his flicked backheel volley in a 4–0 victory over Bastia in 2013!

TOP TRICKS

Neymar
PARIS SAINT-GERMAIN v Toulouse

Shortly after his £200 million move to PSG, Neymar showed off all his skills and tricks with a slick finish. The Brazilian rode four challenges in the area, spun with the ball at his feet and kept control to lash in his team's sixth goal!

Up and over it goes!

LONG-RANGE MASTER
Juninho
LYON v Sedan

Lyon's Brazilian free-kick master shocked the footy world with this goal back in 2008. With the ball positioned a huge 37 metres (40 yards) from Sedan's goal, Juninho blasted it and sent it swerving and bending over the wall. It was utterly mind-blowing!

BIG BEN STRIKES
Hatem Ben Arfa
St-Etienne v NICE

This was a very 'nice' goal in 2015 by the former Newcastle United forward! Ben Arfa dribbled forward and turned past a defender, glided over three tackles and made his way into the box. With his target locked on the goal, the Frenchman whipped a shot bang into the bottom corner.

LYON KING
Memphis Depay
LYON v Toulouse

Former Manchester United forward Depay became a big hero in Ligue 1 with a long-range wonder goal. With the ball in the centre circle, he spun by an opponent and without even looking up, Depay curled a high lobbed shot over the keeper. Pure class!

Depay as you go. Ha. ha!

BEST GOALS EVER!

It may not be as famous as the Premier League or the Bundesliga, but Holland's Eredivisie is still a hotbed of awesome goals and fantastic goalscorers.

KEEPER SURPRISE

Martin Hansen
ADO DEN HAAG v
PSV Eindhoven

Ado Den Haag grabbed a surprise 90th-minute equaliser against Dutch champions PSV. What was even more of a surprise was that it was scored by their keeper, Martin Hansen! He leapt in the box to backheel an amazing goal from a corner.

FEYENOORD ON FIRE

Jens Toornstra
FEYENOORD v
Sparta Rotterdam

This epic Eredivisie goal was a great mix of team work and individual brilliance. Toornstra trapped the ball by the edge of the pitch, played a one-two, took the ball forward on his knee and whipped a wonderful shot over the keeper.

DUTCH DRIBBLING STAR

Steven Bergwijn
Utrecht v PSV Eindhoven

In a 7–1 destruction at Utrecht, the 19-year-old PSV hero Steven Bergwijn scored a super solo goal. The Dutch trickster danced through four challengers and sat the keeper on his bum as he rolled the ball into the goal!

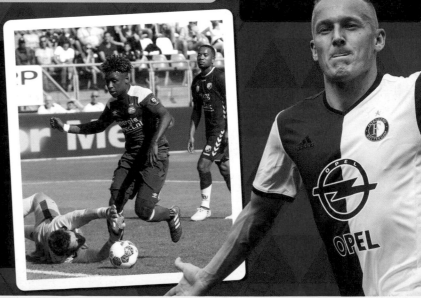

VAN'S VOLLEY

Rafael van der Vaart
AJAX v Feyenoord

Ajax captain Rafael van der Vaart somehow scored a diving backheeled flick against arch-rivals Feyenoord in 2003. The goalscoring midfielder was falling forwards inside the area but flicked his left leg behind him to steer the ball home. The Ajax fans went bonkers!

GOAL-DEN GRONINGEN

Michael De Leeuw
FC GRONINGEN v NEC Nijmegen

De Leeuw blasted a hat-trick as FC Groningen won this game 5–1 in 2013, and his second goal looked impossible to score! He raced to meet a cross in the box, spun in the air and knocked the ball in while facing away from the goal. No one knows how he did it!

Thanks very Dutch!

DRIBBLING DEMBELE

Mousa Dembele
Willem II v AZ ALKMAAR

Tottenham Hotspur's midfield star began his career in the Dutch Eredivisie. His No.1 strike came in 2008 for AZ Alkmaar. Dembele set off on an incredible dribbling drive into the box, beating five challenges and then striking low past the keeper – a special goal!

BEST GOALS EVER!

Portugal's top league is home to huge clubs like Benfica, Porto and Sporting Lisbon – and plenty of jaw-dropping goals!

You ain't stoppin' this, keeps!

EDGAR COSTA
MARITIMO v Nacional

Against their Madeira island rivals Nacional, Maritimo forward Edgar Costa produced the goal of his life! He chested the ball just outside the area, took two clever touches in the air and swivelled to blast an unstoppable volley.

FAB FREE-KICK
Victor Lindelof
Sporting Lisbon v BENFICA

Manchester United hope Victor Lindelof will score goals like this at Old Trafford! The Sweden centre-back crashed a right-footed rocket free-kick past Sporting Lisbon as the Eagles soared to yet another Primeira Liga crown.

PASS MASTERS
Rodrigo Lima
BENFICA v Sporting Lisbon

Benfica midfielder Nicolas Gaitan began a top team move in this high-pressure Primeira Liga game. He tricked past two players, played a quick one-two before looping a ball into the box for Rodrigo Lima to finish with an acrobatic volley. Amazing!

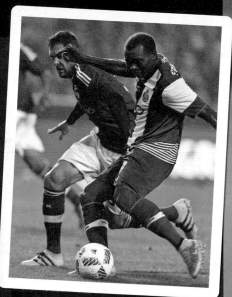

It's Guarin the goal!

PORTO POWER
Vincent Aboubakar
Benfica v PORTO

In 2016, Porto worked a great team goal against title rivals Benfica. Quick one-touch passing between three players released striker Vincent Aboubakar into the box and he controlled the ball before rocketing a match winner!

OVER THE MOON

Salvador Agra
NACIONAL v Maritimo

Agra's outrageous overhead kick in Nacional's derby game with Maritimo sent the fans wild! The winger rose into the air to angle an accurate kick back across the goal in a famous 2–0 win for his team.

FREDY'S READY
Fredy Guarin
PORTO v Maritimo

Even though he was more than 30 metres (33 yards) away from the goal, Porto's Colombian midfielder Guarin smashed a superb Primeira Liga piledriver! It was one of the best strikes of the 2010–11 season as Porto finished 21 points clear at the top of the table.

BEST GOALS EVER!

The first FA Cup final was in 1872 and there have been hundreds of top goals scored in this famous competition. Here are the best of the best!

SINCLAIR STUNNER

Trevor Sinclair
QUEENS PARK RANGERS v Barnsley
Sinclair was a master of stunning overhead and scissor-kick goals. Playing for QPR in 1997, the winger met a cross in the box by flying in the air and wrapping his right foot around the ball. One of the FA Cup's ultimate goals!

STEVIE'S SCREAMER

Steven Gerrard
LIVERPOOL v West Ham United
The Reds skipper had already scored a cracker in the 2006 FA Cup final, but his second goal was even better! In the 90th minute, with Liverpool losing 3–2, he bashed it in from long range as Gerrard's team went on to win the final on penalties.

SEMI SCREAMER

Ryan Giggs
Arsenal v MANCHESTER UNITED
In extra-time of a dramatic FA Cup semi-final replay in 1999, Manchester United winger Giggs unleashed the finest goal of his awesome career. The Welshman collected the ball in his own half and dribbled into Arsenal area and won the game with a lethal left-foot shot!

VILLA'S VICTORY

Ricky Villa
TOTTENHAM HOTSPUR v Manchester City

Spurs won the FA Cup in 1981, but only after Argentina star Ricky Villa helped them beat Manchester City in a final replay. He showed amazing technique and skill to dribble into the box, skip four tackles and slot the ball into the net at Wembley!

FOREST THUMP GUNNERS!

Eric Lichaj
NOTTINGHAM FOREST v Arsenal

Eric Lichaj scored twice in the first half during Nottingham Forest's mega 4–2 win against the FA Cup champions. His second was a sweet strike as he looped a precise volley over David Ospina after expert control on his chest.

Alonso scored for **Liverpool FC** in their 2005 Champions League final win over AC Milan.

ACE ALONSO

Xabi Alonso
Luton v LIVERPOOL

Another quality goal from Liverpool's fantastic 2006 FA Cup campaign! Beating Luton 4–3, Spain star Alonso curled the ball into an empty net with a left-foot drive from well inside his own area. It trickled over the line to seal a 5–3 victory.

5 WAYS TO...
SCORE A PENALTY

Power-packed, precise or a cheeky chip – there are many ways to convert a top-class penalty. Scan these tips and tricks to help you score from the spot.

Kane scored his 100th goal in the Premier League from a penalty.

1

If you aim to kick the ball against the side netting of the goal, you'll have a greater chance of scoring. This could mean that you curl the ball away from the keeper using the inside part of your foot. You'll still need to hit the ball quite hard so that it has the speed to beat the keeper.

JUST LIKE... Harry Kane
(Tottenham Hotspur)

2

Making the keeper think you'll shoot one way, then shooting the other is the secret to scoring a penalty! For example, if you're about to side-foot the ball to your left, try twisting your body in the other direction and placing your shot to the right at the last second. This will take lots of non-match practice!

JUST LIKE... Cristiano Ronaldo
(Real Madrid)

3

Make sure you take lots of practice free-kicks, either in training or in kickabouts at home or school. A good tip is to try beating a keeper from slightly further away than your usual penalty-spot distance. Then, when you come to taking a kick from the proper spot, it'll seem much easier!

JUST LIKE... Jonjo Shelvey
(Newcastle United)

Penalty takers can choose to kick to the right, the left, go high or low and even blast straight ahead. But perhaps the most famous, and cheekiest, technique is to coolly chip the ball down the middle. This is known as the 'panenka' penalty.

JUST LIKE... Eden Hazard
(Chelsea)

4

Be confident when you chip.

5

As long as the ball is hit forwards, and the penalty taker doesn't strike it twice, you can 'pass' from a spot kick. Against Celta Vigo in 2016, Lionel Messi slowly rolled the ball forwards from a penalty and Luis Suarez scored after racing into the box.

JUST LIKE... Lionel Messi & Luis Suarez
(Barcelona)

EPIC OWN GOALS!

Is there anything worse (or funnier) than scoring against your own team? Check out these total fails as players hit epic own goals!

BURY BRUISER

What an epic fail! In 2006, Bury defender Chris Brass tried to clear the ball by kicking it over his head. But, it smashed him in the face and flew into his own net. He bruised his nose too. Ouch!

TRICKY TRAORE

In the FA Cup in 2005, Liverpool defender Djimi Traore scored an OG at Burnley by spinning on the ball and flicking it in. It would have been a great goal... in the right end!

SLAM DUNK

Brighton & Hove Albion centre-back Lewis Dunk chested and juggled the ball on his knee before knocking the ball into his goal. Liverpool FC were very happy with his goal skills!

I've gotta face facts!

BAD KOMPANY

He's won three Premier League crowns, but Vincent Kompany also wins Manchester City's worst OG award! At Fulham in 2013, he swung at the ball which looped off his boot and over Joe Hart's head.

OH NO, DABO

While on loan at Vitesse Arnhem from Chelsea, defender Fankaty Dabo lofted an ace own goal from the touchline right over the keeper!

INTER THE GOAL

Inter Milan's Geoffrey Kondogbia scored an own goal from near the centre circle against Chelsea. It could be the greatest long-distance OG ever!

GUNNER HATE IT!

Look away now, Arsenal fans! Defender Carl Jenkinson lobbed a ridiculous volley into the Arsenal net in 2011. It was the most impressive he ever scored at the club!

Epic fail!

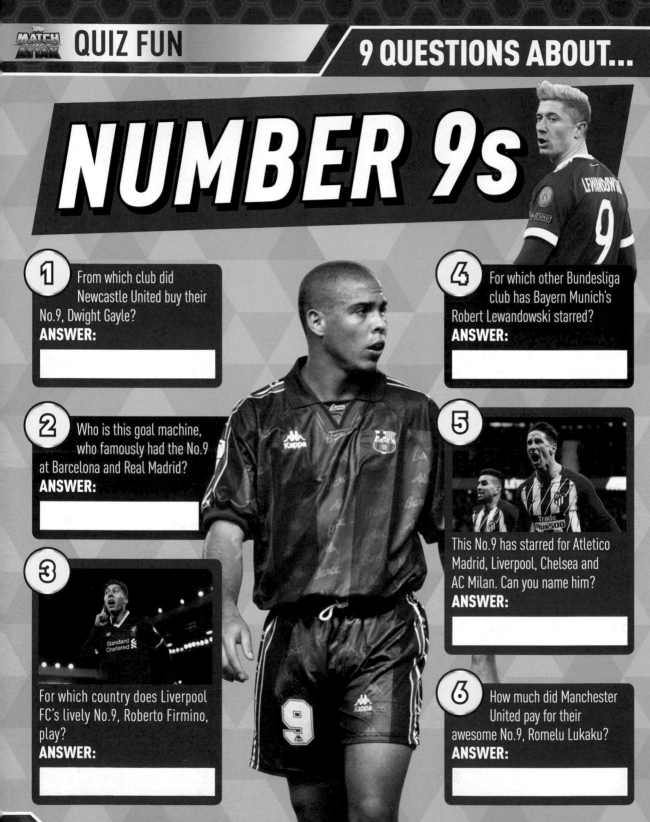

NUMBER 9s

1 From which club did Newcastle United buy their No.9, Dwight Gayle?

ANSWER:

2 Who is this goal machine, who famously had the No.9 at Barcelona and Real Madrid?

ANSWER:

3 For which country does Liverpool FC's lively No.9, Roberto Firmino, play?

ANSWER:

4 For which other Bundesliga club has Bayern Munich's Robert Lewandowski starred?

ANSWER:

5 This No.9 has starred for Atletico Madrid, Liverpool, Chelsea and AC Milan. Can you name him?

ANSWER:

6 How much did Manchester United pay for their awesome No.9, Romelu Lukaku?

ANSWER:

7 In which season did Leicester City striker Jamie Vardy win the Premier League title?

ANSWER:

8

Who is this record-breaking Paris Saint-Germain striker?

ANSWER:

9 Which popular Manchester United No.9 scored five in the club's record 9–0 Premier League win against Ipswich Town?

ANSWER:

That's a 'vard' question to answer!

In 2012, **Vardy** joined Leicester City for a bargain £1 million from Fleetwood Town!

VARDY

9

Pages 18–19
Spot the Strikers

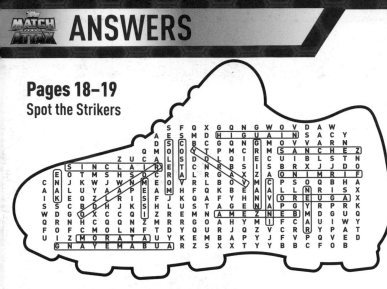

Pages 44–45 Goal Guessing
1. Goal, 2. Goal, 3. Not a goal, 4. Not a goal, 5. Not a goal.

Pages 66–67 Goal Grids

How well did you score?

Pages 78–79 Spot the Difference

1.

2.

3.

4.

Pages 92–93 Number 9s
1. Crystal Palace, 2. Ronaldo, 3. Brazil,
4. Borussia Dortmund, 5. Fernando Torres,
6. a reported £75 million, 7. 2015–16,
8. Edinson Cavani, 9. Andrew Cole.